599.5   Keogh, Josie
KEO   What are sea mammals?

**ANNIE E VINTON ELEMENTARY
SCHOOL LIBRARY
306 STAFFORD ROAD
MANSFIELD CENTER, CT 06250**

WHAT ARE SEA MAMMALS?

JOSIE KEOGH

Britannica®
Educational Publishing

IN ASSOCIATION WITH

ROSEN
EDUCATIONAL SERVICES

Published in 2017 by Britannica Educational Publishing (a trademark of Encyclopædia Britannica, Inc.) in association with The Rosen Publishing Group, Inc.
29 East 21st Street, New York, NY 10010

Distributed exclusively by Rosen Publishing.
To see additional Britannica Educational Publishing titles, go to rosenpublishing.com.

First Edition

Britannica Educational Publishing
J.E. Luebering: Executive Director, Core Editorial
Mary Rose McCudden: Editor, Britannica Student Encyclopedia

Rosen Publishing
Bernadette Davis: Editor
Nelson Sá: Art Director
Brian Garvey: Designer
Cindy Reiman: Photography Manager
Sherri Jackson: Photo Researcher

Library of Congress Cataloging-in-Publication Data

Names: Keogh, Josie, author.
Title: What are sea mammals? / Josie Keogh.
Description: First edition. | New York : Britannica Educational Publishing in association with Rosen Educational Services, 2017. | Series: Let's find out! Marine life | Audience: Grades 1 to 4. | Includes bibliographical references and index.
Identifiers: LCCN 2016023861| ISBN 9781680486056 (library bound : alk. paper) | ISBN 9781508103912 (pbk. : alk. paper) | ISBN 9781508103158 (6-pack : alk. paper)
Subjects: LCSH: Marine mammals—Juvenile literature.
Classification: LCC QL713.2 .K46 2017 | DDC 599.5—dc23
LC record available at https://lccn.loc.gov/2016023861

Manufactured in China

Photo credits: Cover, p. 1, interior pages background image Willyam Bradberry/Shutterstock.com; p. 4 © outdoorsman/Fotolia; pp. 4–5 © Nicolas Larento/Fotolia; p. 6 Colors and Shapes of underwater world/Moment/Getty Images; p. 7 Danita Delimont/Gallo Images/Getty Images; p. 8 Werner Van Steen/The Image Bank/Getty Images; pp. 9, 21 Encyclopædia Britannica, Inc.; p. 10 Nagel Photography/Shutterstock.com; pp. 10–11 Dan Kitwood/Getty Images; p. 12 Jan Zoetekouw/Hemera/Thinkstock; p. 13 Matt9122/Shutterstock.com; p. 14 © Photos.com/Thinkstock; p. 14–15 jamirae/iStock/Thinkstock; p. 16 © Marcel Hurni/Fotolia; p. 17 © desertrends/Fotolia; p. 18 James Watt/U.S. Department of the Interior; p. 19 Francisco Erize/Bruce Coleman Ltd.; p. 20 Jeff Foott; p. 22 Therese Flanagan/Moment/Getty Images; p. 23 Wayne R Bilenduke/Stone/Getty Images; p. 24 David Courtenay/Oxford Scientific/Getty Images; p. 25 Shane Anderson/NOAA; p. 26 Timothy Allen/Photonica World/Getty Images; p. 27 Andrew Lichtenstein/Corbis Historical/Getty Images; p. 28 © corepics/Fotolia; p. 29 © Lisa Lubin - www.llworldtour.com(A Britannica Publishing Partner).

CONTENTS

LIFE IN THE OCEAN

While fish can spend their whole lives under the water's surface, whales have to rise to the surface to breathe. This is because whales—unlike fish—are mammals.

A mammal is an animal that breathes air, has a backbone, and grows hair at some point during its life. All female mammals can produce milk for their young. Animals within this

Humpback whales are very acrobatic marine mammals. They often leap out of the water and then arch backward as they fall back down.

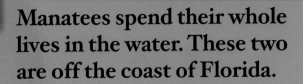
Manatees spend their whole lives in the water. These two are off the coast of Florida.

group are among the most intelligent of all living creatures. Humans are a part of this group. Mammals that live in the world's oceans are called marine mammals. Whales are marine mammals. So are seals, sea lions, walruses, manatees, polar bears, and sea otters. Some marine mammals, such as whales, live their whole lives in the water. Others, such as polar bears, spend part of their time on land.

COMPARE AND CONTRAST

Whales and sharks both live in oceans, but whales are marine mammals and sharks are fish. Compare and contrast the two.

WHAT MAKES A MAMMAL?

Mammals are the only animals that make milk to nourish their young. The female has special **glands** called mammary glands. After childbirth, the mother's glands produce milk. The mother feeds the young with this milk until the young are old enough to get

This baby manatee is drinking its mother's milk. Manatee mothers and calves communicate with sounds. They make chirps, squeaks, and grunts.

food for themselves. Marine mammal milk has a lot of fat in it. This helps the babies grow quickly.

All mammals have hair at some stage of development. Some marine mammals have more than others. For example, the thick fur coat of sea otters keeps them warm in the cold waters where they live. On the other hand, whales have very little hair. Some whales have hair only before they are born. A thick layer of fat, called blubber, keeps them warm instead. Some marine mammals, such as fur seals, have both thick coats and blubber.

Sea otters have the thickest fur of any animal. Their coats have a soft undercoat and longer guard hairs.

Mammals are warm-blooded. This means that they are able to keep their body at roughly the same temperature no matter what the surrounding temperature is. This allows marine mammals to live in waters with a wide range of temperatures.

All mammals breathe air. They use the oxygen in the air to make the energy their bodies need. The bodies of marine mammals can store extra oxygen. This lets them hold their breath for a long time underwater. They still

Some marine mammals live alone, while others, such as walruses, live in groups. Animals that live in groups are social.

Sperm whales are very large, with big heads. They dive down deep into the ocean to find food, such as giant squid.

need to visit the surface to breathe, though.

Mammals have highly developed brains. Their complex brains allow mammals to learn from experience and adapt their behavior. Scientists who study animals have discovered that whales are among the smartest mammals.

sperm whale
(*Physeter catodon*)
length up to 19 m (62 ft)

3 metres

9 feet

Calves, Pups, and Cubs

Marine mammals reproduce through mating. Females carry the developing young in their bodies after mating. The young develop inside a part of their mothers' bodies called the uterus. They receive nutrition through their mothers' bodies.

Gestation, or the length of time that the mother carries the young in the uterus, varies between

While most marine mammals only have one baby at a time, polar bears most often have two.

species, or types. Most whales are pregnant from 9 to 12 months. Marine mammals give birth to live young. Most marine mammals give birth to just one young at a time.

Whale, dolphin, manatee, and dugong babies are called calves. Baby seals, sea lions, walruses, and sea otters are pups, while baby polar bears are cubs. These, as well as other young mammals, learn many behaviors from their parents.

COMPARE AND CONTRAST
Whales and manatees are born underwater, while seals, walruses, and polar bears are born on land. What are the advantages of each place?

Seal pups are born on land. They stay on land until they have grown big enough to stay warm and float in the water.

THE WHALE FAMILY

Whales make up an order, or large group of animals, called Cetacea. This order includes dolphins and porpoises. People often confuse dolphins and porpoises, although dolphins are usually larger and have longer, beaklike snouts. Whales live in oceans around the world. Large species often

There are six species of porpoises. They include the harbor porpoise, the finless porpoise, and the Dall porpoise.

migrate long distances. The shape of a whale's body helps it to move quickly through the water. It pushes its tail up and down to move. The tail is divided into two broad sections called flukes. Whales steer with their flippers.

VOCABULARY

Animals that **migrate** regularly move from one place to another for food or to have babies.

There are two basic kinds of whale: toothed and baleen. Toothed whales have sharp teeth and eat mainly fish and squid. There are about 70 species of toothed whale. These include sperm whales, belugas, killer whales, narwhals, beaked whales, and pilot whales. Dolphins and porpoises also belong to this group.

Bottlenose dolphins live in oceans around the world. Their name comes from their long beaks.

This blue whale is surfacing to breathe. Blue whales are Earth's largest animals.

There are about 10 species of baleen whale. These include blue whales, gray whales, fin whales, humpback whales, sei whales, and right whales. Instead of teeth, these whales have blade-shaped plates, called baleen, hanging from the roof of the mouth. The inner sides of the baleen have bristles that trap food. A baleen whale feeds either by swimming with its mouth open or by gulping water. The baleen acts as a filter, letting out water but holding in small fish, shrimp, and other creatures.

Whales make many sounds, including whistles, barks, and screams, to communicate with other whales.

COMPARE AND CONTRAST

Whales take in air through openings, called blowholes, on the top of their heads. How does this compare with how people breathe?

Toothed whales make special sounds to locate objects they cannot see. These sounds bounce off solid surfaces and travel back to the whale's sensitive ears. This process is called echolocation.

Killer whales are toothed whales. They are also known as orcas.

SEALS AND WALRUSES

Seals can be divided into two groups: earless seals and eared seals. Earless seals actually do have ears, but they do not stick out. Eared seals have **visible** ears. Sea lions are eared seals with a thick, hairy neck that looks like a lion's mane. Fur seals are a

VOCABULARY

Visible things can be seen.

These sea lions are in the Galapagos Islands. Most sea lions live in the Pacific Ocean.

Sea lions range in color from golden brown to brown to dark brown.

species of eared seal that are known for their thick coats.

Seals are related to walruses. A walrus looks like a big seal with two large upper teeth called tusks. These tusks stick down from the walrus's mouth.

Instead of legs, seals and walruses have two pairs of flippers. The flippers help them swim. Eared seals and walruses can turn their rear flippers forward under the body. This allows them to scoot around while on land. Earless seals cannot turn their rear flippers forward. They move on land by wriggling on their bellies or pulling themselves forward with their front flippers.

Seals are found throughout the world. They are especially common in seas near the North and South poles. Some species like the open ocean. Others prefer to live along the coast. All seals spend some time on islands,

There are more than thirty species of seals. This one is a Hawaiian monk seal. It lives in the waters around Hawaii.

THINK ABOUT IT

Male seals often fight each other over the right to mate with females. How do you think these animals fight?

Male Pacific walruses are slightly larger than females, with longer tusks.

beaches, or sheets of ice. They come ashore to breed.

Seals eat mostly fish. Some also eat squid and shellfish. The leopard seal of the Antarctic feeds on penguins and other seals.

Walruses live in the cold Arctic seas of Europe, Asia, and North America. Walruses eat mostly clams. They dig clams from the seafloor with their tusks. They shovel food into the mouth with their whiskers. Walruses live in groups that can include more than 100 animals. They spend most of their time in the sea, but they sometimes rest on ice or rocky islands.

MANATEES AND DUGONGS

Manatees and dugongs look very similar. This is because they are closely related. However, there are some differences. Manatees have flat, rounded tails. As with whales and dolphins, the dugong has a deeply notched tail, or fluke.

Both animals live in warm coastal waters. However, the dugong lives in the Indian and Pacific oceans, while most manatees live in the Atlantic Ocean.

Caribbean manatees, like these, are found in Florida and the West Indies.

dugong
(*Dugong dugon*)
average length 2.7 m (9 ft)

Dugongs have broad snouts with bristles, or thick hairs.

Some manatees also live in South America's Amazon River.

Manatees and dugongs are slow-moving, peaceful animals. Unlike most other marine mammals, they are herbivores, or plant eaters. They use their flippers to push the food toward their mouths.

Manatees live alone or in small family groups. Dugongs are most often seen alone or in pairs. Herds of 100–200 dugongs, however, are sometimes seen.

COMPARE AND CONTRAST

Manatees and dugongs have a lot in common. In what ways are they alike? How are they different?

POLAR BEARS

Polar bears are excellent swimmers. They are large, powerful hunters with no natural predators.

Polar bears live in Earth's Arctic regions, so they spend a lot of their time on sea ice. They can travel long distances on the ice floes that drift through Arctic waters.

Polar bears mostly live alone. They feed mainly

THINK ABOUT IT

Can you think of any way that a polar bear's white coat might be an advantage?

on sea mammals, especially seals. They are good hunters, but they also will eat dead fish, stranded whales, and even garbage. Polar bears hunt both on the ice and in the water. They are good but unusual swimmers: they use only their front legs to swim.

In winter, a female polar bear gives birth in a snowy den. She has one to four tiny cubs at a time. She nurses them for about two years. After they are weaned, cubs stay with their mother for a few more years, until they are ready to mate.

Polar bear cubs spend their first few months in their den and come out only when spring has finally arrived.

SEA OTTERS

Sea otters are well-suited to ocean life. Their webbed feet are good for swimming. Unlike many animals, sea otters can safely drink salt water. This allows them to remain at sea for several days at a time.

Sea otters live along the Pacific Coast of North America. They are usually solitary but are sometimes seen in groups. Gatherings of up to 2,000

VOCABULARY

Solitary animals spend most of their time alone.

This sea otter is eating a sea urchin. Sea urchins are an important food for these marine mammals.

Sea otters play a key role in protecting the kelp forests that grow off the west coast of North America. Kelp is a large kind of seaweed.

have been seen along the coast of Alaska. At night, sea otters may choose either to sleep on land or simply to float near beds of seaweed. Sea otters eat sea urchins, crabs, shellfish, and fish. They usually eat while floating on their backs. They often use rocks to break open crabs and shellfish. They crush sea urchins with their forefeet and teeth. Female sea otters give birth to one pup in the water. The pup remains dependent on its mother for six to eight months.

Threats to Marine Mammals

People have hunted marine mammals for the animals' meat, hides, blubber, and fur for thousands of years. Several species of large whales became endangered, or in danger of dying out. Sea otters and seal species that were hunted for their fur also became endangered. In the 20th century, countries passed laws protecting marine mammals. This has helped the animals make a comeback.

Tanneries are places where people make leather from animal skins. Leather is one of many products people get from the animals they hunt.

Still, people continue to do things that threaten marine mammals. Many manatees have been hurt or killed by boat propellers. Pollution is a problem, too. It can make marine mammals sick and kill off the animals or plants they depend on for food. Oil spills hurt all marine mammals but are especially bad for sea otters. When the oil covers their fur, the otters' coats cannot keep them warm.

Water pollution is a threat to marine mammals, such as this dolphin.

THINK ABOUT IT

One way to fight global warming is to drive cars less. What are other things people can do to fight global warming?

Global warming—the slow increase in the average temperature on Earth—causes problems, too. When people burn oil, gas, and coal to power factories, run cars, and produce electricity, certain gases are released into Earth's atmosphere. These gases trap the sun's heat and keep Earth warm. Too many of these gases in the atmosphere results in too much of the sun's heat being trapped.

The power plants that produce the energy we use also add to global warming.

Melting glaciers will likely cause changes in ocean temperatures and ocean currents.

Global warming makes sea ice in the Arctic melt. Less sea ice means that polar bears have less space to hunt and to mate. Melting ice could also make sea levels rise. Higher water levels and warmer water temperatures threaten all life in the ocean. People need to work together to improve the environment and to keep marine mammals safe.

GLOSSARY

antarctic The south pole; something that is in or from the south pole.

arctic The north pole; something that is in or from the north pole.

atmosphere The whole mass of air surrounding Earth.

blubber The fat of whales and other large sea mammals.

echolocation A process for locating distant or invisible objects by means of sound waves reflected back to the sender from the objects.

environment An open or closed area where creatures and plants live and interact.

flipper A broad flat limb (of a seal or whale) used for swimming.

fluke One of the two parts of a whale's or dugong's tail.

hide The skin of an animal.

marine In or from the sea.

nourish To provide with food.

organ A body part that consists of cells and tissues and is specialized to do a particular task.

oxygen A gas that is found in the air and is necessary for the survival of all plants and animals.

predator An animal or plant that hunts its food.

sea urchin Round sea animals with spines that live on the sea floor.

species A class of things of the same kind and with the same name.

temperature A measure of how hot or cold something is.

weaned No longer relying on its mother's milk.

webbed Having fingers or toes joined by webs.

For More Information

Books

Butterworth, Christine. *See What a Seal Can Do* (Read and Wonder). Somerville, MA: Candlewick Press, 2015.

Lourie, Peter. *The Manatee Scientists: Saving Vulnerable Species* (Scientists in the Field Series). Boston, MA: HMH Books for Young Readers, 2016.

Marsh, Laura. *National Geographic Readers: Sea Otters*. Washington, DC: National Geographic Children's Books, 2014.

Pringle, Laurence. *Whales!: Strange and Wonderful*. Honesdale, PA: Boyds Mills Press, 2012.

Sill, Cathryn. *About Marine Mammals: A Guide for Children*. Atlanta, GA: Peachtree Publishers, 2016.

Websites

Because of the changing nature of internet links, Rosen Publishing has developed an online list of websites related to the subject of this book. This site is updated regularly. Please use this link to access the list:

http://www.rosenlinks.com/LFO/mammal

Index